HEALTHY RECIPES

FOR THE HOLIDAYS

Pineapple Ginger Shrimp Cocktail .4

Southern Crab Cakes with Rémoulade Dipping Sauce 6

Cranberry-Lime Margarita Punch 8

Pear and Cranberry Salad 10

Crab Cobb Salad 12

Double Corn & Cheddar Chowder 14

Spinach Salad with Hot Apple Dressing 16

Roast Turkey with Cranberry Stuffing 18

Oven-Roasted Boston Scrod 21

Hoppin' John Supper 24

Hazelnut-Coated Salmon Steaks 26

Potato Pancakes with Apple-Cherry Chutney 28

Spicy Southwestern Vegetable Sauté 30

PINEAPPLE GINGER SHRIMP COCKTAIL

Combining the tropical treasures of pineapple and ginger with America's favorite shellfish results in a delectable taste sensation. Cooked, shelled shrimp should look succulent and plump with no hint of ammonia odor. Fresh pineapple spears are available in the produce section of most supermarkets.

9 fresh pineapple spears (about 1 package), divided
¼ cup all-fruit apricot preserves
1 tablespoon finely chopped onion
½ teaspoon grated fresh ginger

⅛ teaspoon ground black pepper
8 ounces cooked medium shrimp (about 30)
1 red or green bell pepper, cut into 12 strips

1 Chop 3 pineapple spears into bite-sized pieces; combine with preserves, onion, ginger and black pepper in medium bowl.

2 Evenly arrange shrimp, bell pepper strips and remaining pineapple spears on 6 small plates lined with lettuce leaves, if desired. Add one spoonful of pineapple mixture to each plate.   *Makes 6 servings*

Nutrients per Serving:

Calories	108 (6% calories from fat)				
Total Fat	1 g	Carbohydrate	20 g	Iron	2 mg
Saturated Fat	trace	Dietary Fiber	2 g	Vitamin A	264 RE
Cholesterol	58 mg	Protein	7 g	Vitamin C	95 mg
Sodium	69 mg	Calcium	24 mg	Sugar	7 g

DIETARY EXCHANGES: 1 Lean Meat, ½ Fruit, 1 Vegetable

SOUTHERN CRAB CAKES WITH RÉMOULADE DIPPING SAUCE

10 ounces fresh lump crabmeat
1½ cups fresh white or sourdough bread crumbs, divided
¼ cup chopped green onions
½ cup nonfat or reduced-fat mayonnaise, divided
2 tablespoons coarse grain or spicy brown mustard, divided

¾ teaspoon hot pepper sauce, divided
1 egg white, lightly beaten
2 teaspoons olive oil, divided
Lemon wedges

1 Preheat oven to 200°F. Combine crabmeat, ¾ cup bread crumbs and green onions in medium bowl. Add ¼ cup mayonnaise, 1 tablespoon mustard, ½ teaspoon pepper sauce and egg white; mix well. Using ¼ cup mixture per cake, shape eight ½-inch-thick cakes. Roll crab cakes lightly in remaining ¾ cup bread crumbs.

2 Heat large nonstick skillet over medium heat until hot; add 1 teaspoon oil. Add 4 crab cakes; cook 4 to 5 minutes per side or until golden brown. Transfer to serving platter; keep warm in oven. Repeat with remaining 1 teaspoon oil and crab cakes.

3 To prepare dipping sauce, combine remaining ¼ cup mayonnaise, 1 tablespoon mustard and ¼ teaspoon pepper sauce in small bowl; mix well.

4 Serve warm crab cakes with lemon wedges and dipping sauce.

Makes 8 servings

Nutrients per Serving:

Calories	81 (25% calories from fat)				
Total Fat	2 g	Carbohydrate	8 g	Iron	1 mg
Saturated Fat	trace	Dietary Fiber	trace	Vitamin A	13 RE
Cholesterol	30 mg	Protein	7 g	Vitamin C	1 mg
Sodium	376 mg	Calcium	48 mg	Sugar	trace

DIETARY EXCHANGES: ½ Starch/Bread, 1 Lean Meat

CRANBERRY-LIME MARGARITA PUNCH

This refreshing and festive punch adds sparkle and panache to any occasion.

6 cups water
1 container (12 ounces) frozen
    cranberry juice cocktail
½ cup lime juice

¼ cup sugar
2 cups ice cubes
1 cup ginger ale or tequila
1 lime, sliced

 Combine water, cranberry juice, lime juice and sugar in punch bowl; stir until sugar dissolves.

 Stir in ice cubes, ginger ale and lime; garnish with fresh cranberries, if desired.

Makes 10 servings

Nutrients per Serving:

Calories	97 (0% calories from fat)				
Total Fat	trace	Carbohydrate	25 g	Iron	trace
Saturated Fat	trace	Dietary Fiber	trace	Vitamin A	1 RE
Cholesterol	0 mg	Protein	trace	Vitamin C	32 mg
Sodium	3 mg	Calcium	8 mg	Sugar	7 g

DIETARY EXCHANGES: 1½ Fruit

❖

Cook's Tip

Add a festive touch to your holidays by adding a colorful and appealing ice ring to your punch bowl. Simply fill a ring mold with some punch and fresh cranberries, freeze until solid, unmold and float the ice ring in the punch bowl.

❖

PEAR AND CRANBERRY SALAD

Bring a touch of elegance to the holidays and create a medley of robust flavors. Be sure to use ripe pears; Forelles and Red Bartletts are particularly well suited for use in this salad. A high-quality balsamic vinegar is a wonderful addition to your pantry.

½ cup canned whole berry cranberry sauce
2 tablespoons balsamic vinegar
1 tablespoon olive or canola oil
12 cups (9 ounces) packed assorted bitter or gourmet salad greens

6 small or 4 large pears (about 1¾ pounds)
2 ounces blue or Gorgonzola cheese, crumbled
Freshly ground black pepper

1 Combine cranberry sauce, vinegar and oil in small bowl; mix well. (Dressing may be covered and refrigerated up to 2 days before serving.)

2 Arrange greens on six serving plates. Cut pears lengthwise into ½-inch-thick slices; cut core and seeds from each slice. Arrange pears attractively over greens. Drizzle cranberry dressing over pears and greens; sprinkle with cheese. Sprinkle with pepper to taste.

Makes 6 servings

Nutrients per Serving:

Calories	161 (29% calories from fat)				
Total Fat	6 g	Carbohydrate	26 g	Iron	1 mg
Saturated Fat	2 g	Dietary Fiber	2 g	Vitamin A	313 RE
Cholesterol	7 mg	Protein	4 g	Vitamin C	20 mg
Sodium	165 mg	Calcium	122 mg	Sugar	1 g

DIETARY EXCHANGES: 2 Fruit, 1 Fat

CRAB COBB SALAD

Fresh or pasteurized crabmeat can be substituted for the canned variety. Crabmeat should always smell fresh and sweet; lump and backfin meat are the best kinds.

12 cups washed and torn
    romaine lettuce
2 cans (6 ounces each)
    crabmeat, drained
2 cups diced ripe tomatoes or
    halved cherry tomatoes
¼ cup (1½ ounces) crumbled
    blue or Gorgonzola cheese

¼ cup cholesterol-free bacon
    bits
¾ cup fat-free Italian or Caesar
    salad dressing
Freshly ground black pepper

 Cover large serving platter with lettuce. Arrange crabmeat, tomatoes, blue cheese and bacon bits attractively over lettuce.

 Just before serving, drizzle dressing evenly over salad; toss well. Transfer to 8 chilled serving plates; sprinkle with pepper to taste.

Makes 8 servings

Nutrients per Serving:

Calories	110 (27% calories from fat)				
Total Fat	3 g	Carbohydrate	8 g	Iron	2 mg
Saturated Fat	1 g	Dietary Fiber	2 g	Vitamin A	262 RE
Cholesterol	46 mg	Protein	12 g	Vitamin C	31 mg
Sodium	666 mg	Calcium	75 mg	Sugar	3 g

DIETARY EXCHANGES: 1½ Lean Meat, 1½ Vegetable

❖

Cook's Tip

This salad can be covered and refrigerated up to five hours before serving. Toss with dressing immediately before serving.

❖

DOUBLE CORN & CHEDDAR CHOWDER

You'll swear you're in the heartland of the Midwest when you indulge in this soup—it's so rich and creamy your family and friends won't believe it's low in fat and cholesterol. Replace some of the chicken broth with light beer to produce a truly authentic Wisconsin specialty.

1 tablespoon margarine
1 cup chopped onion
2 tablespoons all-purpose flour
2½ cups fat-free reduced-sodium chicken broth
1 can (16 ounces) cream-style corn
1 cup frozen whole kernel corn

½ cup finely diced red bell pepper
½ teaspoon hot pepper sauce
¾ cup (3 ounces) shredded sharp Cheddar cheese
Freshly ground black pepper (optional)

1 Melt margarine in large saucepan over medium heat. Add onion; cook and stir 5 minutes. Sprinkle onion with flour; cook and stir 1 minute.

2 Add chicken broth; bring to a boil, stirring frequently. Add cream-style corn, corn kernels, bell pepper and pepper sauce; bring to a simmer. Cover; simmer 15 minutes.

3 Remove from heat; gradually stir in cheese until melted. Ladle into soup bowls; sprinkle with black pepper, if desired.   *Makes 6 servings*

Double Corn, Cheddar & Rice Chowder: Add 1 cup cooked white or brown rice with corn.

Nutrients per Serving:

Calories	180 (28% calories from fat)				
Total Fat	6 g	Carbohydrate	28 g	Iron	1 mg
Saturated Fat	2 g	Dietary Fiber	2 g	Vitamin A	177 RE
Cholesterol	10 mg	Protein	7 g	Vitamin C	49 mg
Sodium	498 mg	Calcium	88 mg	Sugar	1 g

DIETARY EXCHANGES: 1½ Starch/Bread, ½ Lean Meat, 1 Fat

SPINACH SALAD WITH HOT APPLE DRESSING

*Even though green leafy vegetables, like spinach, are some of the
healthiest foods you can eat, it used to be difficult to make them
appealing and tempting—until now! Turkey bacon offers all the
flavor of regular bacon with nearly half the saturated fat.*

6 strips turkey bacon
¾ cup apple cider
2 tablespoons brown sugar
4 teaspoons rice wine vinegar
¼ teaspoon ground black pepper
6 cups washed and torn spinach
    leaves

2 cups sliced mushrooms
1 medium tomato, cut into
    wedges
½ cup thinly sliced red onion

1 Heat medium nonstick skillet over medium heat until hot; add bacon
and cook 2 to 3 minutes per side or until crisp; remove from pan.
Coarsely chop 3 pieces; set aside. Finely chop remaining 3 pieces; return
to skillet. Add apple cider, sugar, vinegar and pepper. Heat just to a
simmer; remove from heat.

2 Combine spinach, mushrooms, tomato and onion in large bowl. Add
dressing; toss to coat. Top with reserved bacon. *Makes 6 servings*

Nutrients per Serving:

Calories	95 (28% calories from fat)				
Total Fat	3 g	Carbohydrate	14 g	Iron	2 mg
Saturated Fat	1 g	Dietary Fiber	2 g	Vitamin A	389 RE
Cholesterol	9 mg	Protein	5 g	Vitamin C	22 mg
Sodium	256 mg	Calcium	74 mg	Sugar	1 g

DIETARY EXCHANGES: ½ Fruit, 1½ Vegetable, ½ Fat

ROAST TURKEY WITH CRANBERRY STUFFING

A New England twist enlivens this quintessential holiday dish. Taking off the turkey skin eliminates loads of fat without removing any of the succulence.

Cranberry Stuffing (page 44)   1 turkey (8 to 10 pounds)

1 Prepare Cranberry Stuffing. *Reduce oven temperature to 350°F.*

2 Remove giblets from turkey. Rinse turkey and cavity in cold water; pat dry with paper towels. Fill turkey cavity loosely with stuffing. Place remaining stuffing in casserole sprayed with nonstick cooking spray. Cover casserole; refrigerate until baking time.

3 Spray roasting pan with nonstick cooking spray. Place turkey, breast side up, on rack in roasting pan. Bake 3 hours or until thermometer inserted in thickest part of thigh registers 185°F and juices run clear.

4 Transfer turkey to serving platter. Cover loosely with foil; let stand 20 minutes. Place covered casserole of stuffing in oven; *increase oven temperature to 375°F.* Bake 25 to 30 minutes or until hot.

5 Remove and discard turkey skin. Slice turkey and serve with Cranberry Stuffing and Spicy Southwestern Vegetable Sauté (page 66), if desired. Garnish with fresh rosemary sprigs, if desired.

Makes 10 servings

continued on page 20

Roast Turkey with Cranberry Stuffing, continued

CRANBERRY STUFFING

1 loaf (12 ounces) Italian or
   French bread, cut into
   ½-inch cubes
2 tablespoons margarine
1½ cups chopped onions
1½ cups chopped celery
2 teaspoons poultry seasoning
1 teaspoon dried thyme leaves

½ teaspoon dried rosemary
¼ teaspoon salt
¼ teaspoon ground black pepper
1 cup coarsely chopped fresh
   cranberries
1 tablespoon sugar
¾ cup fat-free reduced-sodium
   chicken broth

1 Preheat oven to 375°F. Arrange bread on two 15×10-inch jelly-roll pans. Bake 12 minutes or until lightly toasted.

2 Melt margarine in large saucepan over medium heat. Add onions and celery. Cook and stir 8 minutes or until vegetables are tender; remove from heat. Add bread cubes, poultry seasoning, thyme, rosemary, salt and pepper; mix well. Combine cranberries and sugar in small bowl; mix well. Add to bread mixture; toss well. Drizzle chicken broth evenly over mixture; toss well.

Makes 10 servings

Nutrients per Serving:
(turkey and stuffing)

Calories	439 (26% calories from fat)				
Total Fat	12 g	Carbohydrate	23 g	Iron	5 mg
Saturated Fat	4 g	Dietary Fiber	1 g	Vitamin A	32 RE
Cholesterol	136 mg	Protein	56 g	Vitamin C	4 mg
Sodium	445 mg	Calcium	91 mg	Sugar	2 g

DIETARY EXCHANGES: 1½ Starch/Bread, 6 Lean Meat

OVEN-ROASTED BOSTON SCROD

Scrod, another name for young cod, was introduced at the Parker House Hotel in Boston in the 1890's. Scrod's naturally delicate flavor and flaky texture dominate this easy-to-prepare dish.

½ cup seasoned dry bread crumbs
1 teaspoon grated fresh lemon peel
1 teaspoon dried dill weed
1 teaspoon paprika
3 tablespoons all-purpose flour
2 egg whites

1 tablespoon water
1½ pounds Boston scrod or orange roughy fillets, cut into 6 (4-ounce) pieces
2 tablespoons margarine, melted
Tartar Sauce (page 46)
Lemon wedges

1 Preheat oven to 400°F. Spray 15×10-inch jelly-roll pan with nonstick cooking spray. Combine bread crumbs, lemon peel, dill and paprika in shallow bowl or pie plate. Place flour in resealable plastic food storage bag. Beat egg whites and water together in another shallow bowl or pie plate.

2 Add fish, one fillet at a time, to bag. Seal bag; turn to coat fish lightly. Dip fish into egg white mixture, letting excess drip off. Roll fish in bread crumb mixture. Place in prepared jelly-roll pan. Repeat with remaining fish fillets. Brush margarine evenly over fish. Bake 15 to 18 minutes or until fish begins to flake when tested with fork.

3 Prepare Tartar Sauce while fish is baking. Serve fish with lemon wedges and Tartar Sauce.   *Makes 6 servings*

continued on page 22

Oven-Roasted Boston Scrod, continued

TARTAR SAUCE

½ cup nonfat or reduced-fat
    mayonnaise
¼ cup sweet pickle relish

2 teaspoons Dijon mustard
¼ teaspoon hot pepper sauce
    (optional)

 Combine all ingredients in small bowl; mix well.   *Makes ⅔ cup*

Nutrients per Serving:

Calories	215 (21% calories from fat)				
Total Fat	5 g	Carbohydrate	18 g	Iron	1 mg
Saturated Fat	1 g	Dietary Fiber	trace	Vitamin A	81 RE
Cholesterol	49 mg	Protein	23 g	Vitamin C	2 mg
Sodium	754 mg	Calcium	31 mg	Sugar	trace

DIETARY EXCHANGES: 1 Starch/Bread, 2½ Lean Meat

❖

Health Note
Scrod and cod are naturally low in fat and calories and
high in valuable omega-3 fatty acids.

❖

HOPPIN' JOHN SUPPER

The traditional good luck New Year's Day feast in the South, hoppin' John is brimming with flavor and perfect for holiday festivities.

1 cup uncooked converted white rice
1 can (about 14 ounces) fat-free reduced-sodium chicken broth
¼ cup water
1 package (16 ounces) frozen black-eyed peas, thawed
1 tablespoon vegetable oil
1 cup chopped onion

1 cup diced carrots
¾ cup thinly sliced celery with tops
3 cloves garlic, minced
12 ounces reduced-sodium lean fully cooked ham, cut into ¾-inch pieces
¾ teaspoon hot pepper sauce
½ teaspoon salt

1 Combine rice, chicken broth and water in large saucepan; bring to a boil over high heat. Reduce heat; cover and simmer 10 minutes. Stir in black-eyed peas; cover and simmer 10 minutes or until rice and peas are tender and liquid is absorbed.

2 Meanwhile, heat oil in large skillet over medium heat. Add onion, carrots, celery and garlic; cook and stir 15 minutes or until vegetables are tender. Add ham; heat through. Add hot rice mixture, pepper sauce and salt; mix well. Cover; cook over low heat 10 minutes. Sprinkle with parsley and serve with additional pepper sauce, if desired.

Makes 8 servings

Nutrients per Serving:

Calories	245 (13% calories from fat)					
Total Fat	3 g	Carbohydrate	38 g	Iron		3 mg
Saturated Fat	1 g	Dietary Fiber	4 g	Vitamin A		393 RE
Cholesterol	20 mg	Protein	16 g	Vitamin C		6 mg
Sodium	624 mg	Calcium	42 mg	Sugar		3 g

DIETARY EXCHANGES: 2 Starch/Bread, 1 Lean Meat, 1½ Vegetable

HAZELNUT-COATED SALMON STEAKS

In the United States, hazelnuts (also called filberts) are grown almost exclusively in Oregon, and a single tree will yield nuts for hundreds of years. The skins are bitter, so it is best to remove them.

¼ cup hazelnuts
4 salmon steaks, about 5 ounces
    each
1 tablespoon apple butter

1 tablespoon Dijon mustard
¼ teaspoon dried thyme leaves
⅛ teaspoon ground black pepper
2 cups cooked white rice

 Preheat oven to 375°F. Place hazelnuts on baking sheet; bake 8 minutes or until lightly browned. Quickly transfer nuts to clean dry dish towel. Fold towel; rub vigorously to remove as much of the skins as possible. Finely chop hazelnuts using food processor, nut grinder or chef's knife.

 Increase oven temperature to 450°F. Place salmon in baking dish. Combine apple butter, mustard, thyme and pepper in small bowl. Brush on salmon; top each steak with nuts. Bake 14 to 16 minutes or until salmon flakes easily with fork. Serve with rice and steamed snow peas, if desired.

Makes 4 servings

Nutrients per Serving:

Calories	329 (30% calories from fat)					
Total Fat	11 g	Carbohydrate	26 g	Iron	3 mg
Saturated Fat	1 g	Dietary Fiber	1 g	Vitamin A	45 RE
Cholesterol	72 mg	Protein	31 g	Vitamin C	trace
Sodium	143 mg	Calcium	34 mg	Sugar	trace

DIETARY EXCHANGES: 1½ Starch/Bread, 4 Lean Meat

❖

Health Note

Salmon is one of the richest sources of omega-3 fatty acids. Evidence suggests that these acids may prevent blood clots, lessen arthritis pain and help prevent Alzheimer's disease.

❖

POTATO PANCAKES WITH APPLE-CHERRY CHUTNEY

Apple-Cherry Chutney (recipe follows)
1 pound baking potatoes, about 2 medium
½ small onion
3 egg whites

2 tablespoons all-purpose flour
½ teaspoon salt
¼ teaspoon ground black pepper
4 teaspoons vegetable oil, divided

1 Prepare Apple-Cherry Chutney; set aside.

2 Peel potatoes; cut into chunks. Combine potatoes, onion, egg whites, flour, salt and pepper in food processor or blender; process until almost smooth (mixture will appear grainy).

3 Heat large nonstick skillet 1 minute over medium heat. Add 1 teaspoon oil. Spoon 2 tablespoons batter per pancake into skillet. Cook 3 pancakes at a time, 3 minutes per side or until golden brown. Repeat with remaining batter, adding 1 teaspoon oil with each batch. Serve with Apple-Cherry Chutney.

Makes 1 dozen pancakes (2 pancakes per serving)

APPLE–CHERRY CHUTNEY

1 cup chunky applesauce
½ cup canned tart cherries, drained
2 tablespoons brown sugar

1 teaspoon lemon juice
½ teaspoon ground cinnamon
⅛ teaspoon ground nutmeg

1 Combine all ingredients in small saucepan; bring to a boil. Reduce heat; simmer 5 minutes. Serve warm. *Makes 1½ cups*

Nutrients per Serving:

Calories	164 (17% calories from fat)				
Total Fat	3 g	Carbohydrate	31 g	Iron	1 mg
Saturated Fat	trace	Dietary Fiber	1 g	Vitamin A	17 RE
Cholesterol	0 mg	Protein	4 g	Vitamin C	12 mg
Sodium	214 mg	Calcium	18 mg	Sugar	2 g

DIETARY EXCHANGES: 1½ Starch/Bread, ½ Fruit, ½ Fat

SPICY SOUTHWESTERN VEGETABLE SAUTÉ

The staples of Southwestern cuisine are featured in this mélange of spice and savor. Adding more jalapeño peppers will certainly indulge those with a "fiery" palate.

1 bag (16 ounces) frozen green beans
2 tablespoons water
1 tablespoon olive oil
1 red bell pepper, chopped
1 medium yellow summer squash or zucchini, chopped
1 jalapeño pepper, seeded, chopped*

½ teaspoon garlic powder
½ teaspoon ground cumin
½ teaspoon chili powder
¼ cup sliced green onions
2 tablespoons chopped fresh cilantro (optional)
1 tablespoon brown sugar

1 Heat large skillet over medium heat; add green beans, water and oil. Cover; cook 4 minutes, stirring occasionally.

2 Add bell pepper, squash, jalapeño, garlic powder, cumin and chili powder. Cook uncovered, stirring occasionally, 4 minutes or until vegetables are crisp-tender. Stir in green onions, cilantro, if desired, and brown sugar. *Makes 6 servings*

*Jalapeños can sting and irritate the skin; wear rubber gloves when handling peppers and do not touch eyes. Wash hands after handling.

Nutrients per Serving:

Calories	67 (30% calories from fat)				
Total Fat	3 g	Carbohydrate	11 g	Iron	1 mg
Saturated Fat	trace	Dietary Fiber	2 g	Vitamin A	292 RE
Cholesterol	0 mg	Protein	2 g	Vitamin C	91 mg
Sodium	110 mg	Calcium	40 mg	Sugar	trace

DIETARY EXCHANGES: 2 Vegetable, ½ Fat